THE BOOK OF no WORRIES

A survival guide for growing up

LIZZIE COX

illustrated by TANJA STEVANOVIC

Quarto is the authority on a wide range of topics.

Quarto educates, entertains and enriches the lives of
our readers—enthusiasts and lovers of hands-on living.

www.quartoknows.com

Author: Lizzie Cox
Illustrator: Tanja Stevanovic
Consultant: John Rees
Editor: Catherine Brereton
Designer: Kate Wilson
QED Editors: Carly Madden and Harriet Stone
QED Designer: Victoria Kimonidou

© 2018 Quarto Publishing plc

This edition first published in 2018 by QEB Publishing,
an imprint of The Quarto Group.
6 Orchard Road
Suite 100
Lake Forest, CA 92630
T: +1 949 380 7510
F: +1 949 380 7575
www.QuartoKnows.com

A CIP record for this book is available from the Library of Congress.

ISBN 978 1 91241 399 7

Manufactured in Guangdong, China CC062018

9 8 7 6 5 4 3 2 1

MIX
Paper from
responsible sources
FSC® C008047

CONTENTS

INTRODUCTION

WHAT ARE WORRIES?

Worry. Say the word 10 times fast and it starts to sound made up—but worries are very real. Worries can even seem to be taking over your life if you let them. But what are they? And how can you change worries to "no worries"?

Worrying is thinking about problems—not just actual problems you really have, but also ones that might happen in the future. And thinking about them over and over and over again. Worries can feel like a load of bees buzzing endlessly around your mind, refusing to let you think about anything else.

Why do we worry?

Your brain is always looking ahead for possible danger, difficulties, and problems—it is a way of keeping you safe. In a way, worrying is your brain trying to protect you. But actually, the opposite happens—worries don't actually help with anything, and instead they make you feel worse.

Think about it—worrying about bad things that **MIGHT** happen doesn't change the future. All it does is make you feel bad. In fact, **worrying is pointless!** It wastes your energy, wastes your time, and doesn't actually achieve anything. The first step to tackling worrying is understanding this. Then there are practical ways that you can keep your worries in check, to stay happy and positive.

That's what this book is all about! Growing up can be tough. It's a difficult journey, because there's a lot to deal with—your **changing body**, your **developing brain**, all kinds of **new experiences**, and some **brand new emotions** too.

With all that going on, it would almost be impossible to not worry about something! This book is designed to help. From peer pressure and social media to homework, bullying, sex, family stuff, and more—if you've ever worried about it, it's probably here in this book.

AND... BREATHE: MINDFULNESS

What is mindfulness and how can it help?

Growing up is S-T-R-E-S-S-F-U-L! It can feel as though you're stuck in your own head (aaargh), worrying about all sorts of things–from schoolwork and friends, to crushes and your changing body.

Be present

Learning to be "mindful" can help you handle stress and live life fully. And it's easy–phew! "Mindfulness" is a way of teaching your brain to focus on the moment and be present... thinking about sounds, feelings, and tastes you experience throughout the day, rather than worrying about what happened earlier or what might happen tomorrow.

The best part? You can be mindful anywhere. You don't need any fancy equipment–you can practice mindfulness in your room, outside, or even on the bus!

GIVE IT A TRY RIGHT NOW!

You take thousands of breaths a day, but how many of those do you actually even notice? Probably close to zero, right?

STOP, BREATHE, AND JUST BE.

1. The first step to mindfulness is to concentrate on your breathing.

2. Focus all of your attention on the air flowing in and out of your body. You don't need to take super-deep breaths, just notice your lungs moving as you breathe in and out.

3. As thoughts–whether they're good or bad– pass through your mind, don't ignore them. But don't hang on to them or start examining them either. Send them a mental smile and let them go.

4. Don't panic if you suddenly realize your mind has drifted, and instead you're wondering what's for dinner–just keep bringing your concentration back to your breath moving in and out.

And that's it! Just a few minutes of this every day can make a huge difference when it comes to handling stress.

DID YOU KNOW?

Studies have shown that mindfulness can help create long-term changes to your mood and levels of happiness! It's also been proven to help with concentration, which will be handy when exam time comes a-calling.

SCHOOL

EEEK: STARTING MIDDLE SCHOOL

Starting anything new can be scary, but moving up to middle school is especially daunting, because it's somewhere you'll spend a **LOT** of time. But new is also exciting, so take a few **deep, mindful breaths** and let's talk.

Q: I really like all the teachers at my school now—what if my new teachers are really scary?

A: It's hard leaving teachers you know—and who know you—behind, but give it some time, and your new teachers will become just as much a part of your life as those at your old school.

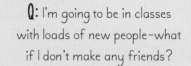

Q: I'm going to be in classes with loads of new people—what if I don't make any friends?

A: The key thing is to be patient. You're probably not going to walk into your first class and suddenly have a whole new squad of best buddies, but that's OK. Everyone's in the same boat—you're all starting a new school together. Forging friendships takes time; be yourself, be friendly, and ask questions to get a conversation started.

4 GREAT THINGS ABOUT STARTING MIDDLE SCHOOL

1 You're growing up!

2 Loads of new stuff to learn–fill that brain with knowledge.

3 New friends (yes, you can still keep your old ones too, don't worry).

4 The chance to stock up on loads of brand new school supplies!

Q: What if the lessons are too hard and I fall behind?

A: As you get older, school subjects do get harder, but the good news is that your brain is developing too (see page 41). Your teachers won't suddenly give you the works of Shakespeare to read overnight, or math problems only a genius could solve–promise! Pay attention in class and do all your homework, and you'll stay on top of things. If you're struggling, tell your teachers– they can help you. That is their job, after all!

AAAARGGH! HOMEWORK AND EXAMS

You know the feeling. You've been working hard all day at school, you get home ready to relax, and **BOOM**, you remember you have a ton of homework or a test to study for. Ugh.

HELPFUL HOMEWORK HINTS

1. **Stay organized.** Spoiler alert: you can't keep on top of schoolwork if you don't know what you need to do! Write down all your assignments in one place and check them regularly.

2. **Prioritize by due date.** You might enjoy English way more than math, but if the math homework is due first, it makes sense to get it out of the way first.

3. **Find the right study environment.** Lying on the floor with the TV on might be fun, but you won't be able to concentrate. Try and find a quiet space to study. Don't keep your phone next to you, either–it's a big distraction!

4. **Treat yourself.** You know what helps with all that homework? A reward. Put on some music, kick a ball, watch your favorite TV show, read a book–anything you enjoy.

Feeling a bit overwhelmed sometimes is normal, but there are ways to keep those schoolwork worries in check. First things first: get it out of the way **ASAP**. Avoiding things we don't **reeeeeally** want to do is an easy trap to fall into, but you'll enjoy doing fun things so much more if the thought of that science homework isn't lurking in the back of your mind.

What if you don't understand the work, and feel like you are doing it all wrong? Well, getting some things wrong is all part of life and of learning–it's why we go to school! But if you really feel like you're struggling, don't muddle through alone. Ask a parent, brother, sister–even a cousin–if they can explain, or talk to your teacher after the class. There's no shame in asking for help!

REALLY RELATABLE REVISION TIPS

1. **Make a study schedule… and stick to it!** Divide your subjects up by topic and decide what you'll study each day.

2. **Keep mindful.** Start each revision session with a few mindful minutes (see page 7).

3. **Have targets and take regular breaks.** Your brain needs regular rests to absorb information, so try short bursts of revision (25-35 minutes) broken up with 10-minute breaks.

4. **Believe in yourself!** Staying positive is key. If you convince yourself that you will fail, that's more likely to happen. Remember: it's never too late to start!

WHAT NEXT? MORE EDUCATION

Thinking about what you're going to do after you leave school is exciting, but it can also be scary. Until that point, your major life decisions have all been made for you... this is really the first time that you'll be able to choose what's next. **EEEK!** The main thing to remember is that there's no "right" or "wrong"—you need to do what feels right for you, and what's going to make you happiest!

Options, options, options

You don't have to go to a four-year university (gasp!). Lots of people choose apprenticeships or practical, skills-based courses instead.

And there's no rush. You still have a good few years before you have to make any decisions, so hold off on the worrying and immerse yourself in all the things that will help you decide later. Try different subjects, learn more about jobs that interest you, talk to adults about what they did. The more information you have, the better.

SHANAY'S STORY: I WENT TO COLLEGE AND I LOVED IT!

History was my favorite subject at school—I love learning about the past. My dad wanted me to study a science, but we had a talk and he understood that I needed to do what I enjoyed the most. Moving away from home was the scariest thing I've ever done, but college has been the best experience. Meeting new people and learning new things—it's amazing!

JAMIE'S STORY: I DID AN APPRENTICESHIP AND IT WAS GREAT!

Most of my friends went to college after school, but that just wasn't for me. Instead, I got on to a plumbing apprenticeship program. This was a combination of training and working, and it was geared towards a job, which is great. It was definitely the right decision for me!

WORRY BUSTER

You can always change your mind! Life is long and many people change subjects or careers several times. Nothing is set in stone: if something isn't making you happy, you can change it!

MENTAL HEALTH

WHAT IS MENTAL HEALTH?

You know what "health" is - it's the physical condition of our bodies, right? If someone is in good health, then they're free from illness or injury. If someone is in ill-health, they're unwell.

Mental health is the same, but it's just about the brain and what's going on inside your head. Mental health includes your emotional, psychological, and social wellbeing, which, put simply, is the way you feel, think, and act.

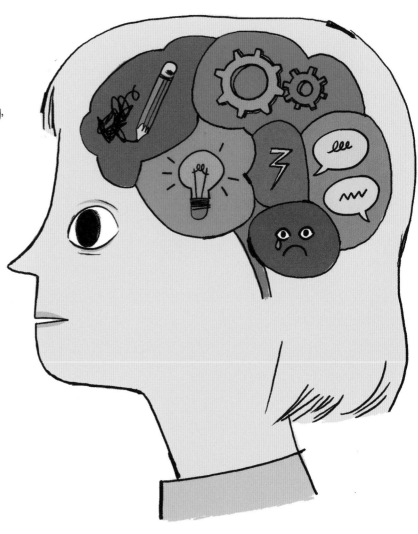

How we feel, think, and act is the foundation of our whole lives as humans, so it's super-important at every stage of growing up– from child, to teen, to adult.

So... what is mental ill-health?

In the same way that we can't control if we get the flu, getting mental ill-health is not a choice. There are all sorts of factors that can contribute: things like the genes you inherit from your family, your upbringing, your life experiences, and your brain chemistry.

Many people experience some form of mental illness at some point in their lives. It's nothing to be ashamed of, not something to joke about, and it's never, ever something you should try to deal with alone.

Just like your body can be unwell in many different ways, so can your mind. Sometimes it, too, needs care, attention, and help from healthcare professionals.

Why is all this important?

Just as exercise can keep us physically fit and healthy, things like having close relationships and talking to friends and family or an adult you trust can keep you emotionally well. Key things to remember are that you are never alone (however much you might feel you are) and that you should never be afraid or embarrassed to ask for help.

You wouldn't walk around with a broken arm without seeing a doctor, would you? Well, the same goes for your mind – if something feels wrong, or bad, you shouldn't suffer in silence. As we've said before, you can always ask for help.

STRESS

You've probably heard adults, in real life or on TV, say "I'm so stressed" or "You're stressing me out!" But not-so-fun fact: stress isn't just a grown-up problem–it can, and does, affect young people too.

What is stress?

Stress is your body and mind's response to pressure or threat, like sitting a big test or taking a free throw in a basketball playoff game.

Physical signs of stress might include your **heartbeat** speeding up, your **knees shaking** or your **palms sweating**. Mentally and emotionally you may feel nervous, on edge, tense, or short-tempered.

Some stress is a natural part of life, but lots of stress over days, weeks, or months can have a serious impact on mental and physical health.

STICK IT TO STRESS

1. Ask yourself: "Will this matter in one year, or even one month?" Taking a moment to look at the big picture helps to keep those worries in check so you don't stress the small stuff.

2. Focus on what can go right, instead of what might go wrong. Imagining all of the worst outcomes will just make you worry more.

3. Remember that you can't control everything. Sometimes, reminding yourself that you can't predict the future or control certain outcomes is comforting.

4. Keep active. Dancing, football, riding your bike-whatever gets you moving, do it. Physical activity is a great way to get you feeling positive.

5. Keep on track. Set yourself targets and focus on one task at a time, to avoid feeling overwhelmed.

6. Sleep, sleep, sleep. Being tired increases stress, so turn that light off and get snoozing!

7. Talk to someone. If you're struggling, the MOST important thing you can do is talk about it. Speak to your teacher, parent, or another trusted adult-they can, and will, help.

ANXIETY AND DEPRESSION

What is anxiety?

Anxiety is a feeling of worry, unease or nervousness. The physical sensations of anxiety are similar to stress: fast heartbeat, shallow breathing, and feeling on edge. Some anxiety is a normal part of life, but many people suffer from anxiety disorders, a type of mental ill-health.

What is an anxiety disorder?

Think about a smoke alarm. The alarm goes off when there's a fire, but sometimes it'll start beeping when there's no danger, like that time your dad burnt the toast. Just like a smoke alarm, anxiety is designed to protect us, but if it goes off all the time, it's not helpful, and can make life miserable. Anxiety disorders can badly affect day-to-day life, making it hard to interact with people or enjoy any activity, because everything feels dangerous and scary.

ELLA'S STORY: LIVING WITH ANXIETY

I didn't realize I had an anxiety disorder—I knew that I worried a lot, but it was more than that. Imagine you've been invited to a party. Someone without an anxiety disorder will look forward to it, even if they feel a bit nervous. Well, I would worry about it for **DAYS**. The thought of walking into the party made me shake and feel like I couldn't breathe—so I didn't go. In fact, I stopped leaving the house for anything but school, and even found that hard. Eventually I realized that this wasn't normal, and I spoke to my mom, who was really brilliant. Now I'm seeing a counsellor, and this has helped a lot.

Depression

It's totally normal to feel down or upset from time to time. However, some people suffer from a serious mental illness, called depression, which is much more than being just sad. People who are depressed find it almost impossible to stop feeling sad and hopeless for months or years at a time. They may struggle to find any enjoyment in any part of life, or feel worthless and unlovable.

For some people depression can be so severe that it can lead to suicidal thoughts–but doctors CAN treat depression, with medication and therapy. If you think that you (or someone close to you) might be depressed, or feel like you want to hurt yourself in some way, speak to someone and let them know how you feel. The first step is knowing that you're not alone, and taking that first step on the road to recovery... even if it feels like you'll never get there. You will.

FRIENDS

HOW TO COPE WITH BULLYING

Being bullied is something that, sadly, many young people have to deal with. It can make you feel alone, sad, left out, and hopeless. It can even lead to mental ill-health problems like anxiety, depression, and wanting to hurt yourself.

Bullying takes many forms. It can be physical, like someone hurting you, or emotional, like being excluded from a friendship group or being made fun of. It can happen face to face or online. But all forms of bullying are **not** OK.

If you are being bullied, tell a teacher what's going on. Also, anti-bullying organizations (see page 63) offer advice and support.

WORRY BUSTER

Is friendship supposed to feel like this? There's a **BIG** difference between a bit of teasing or falling out with friends, and deliberate and repeated bullying. A healthy, real friendship should **NOT** make you regularly feel bad about yourself, constantly worry if you are liked, or be hard work most of the time. It should **NEVER** make you feel like you have to do or say things you don't want to.

KYLE'S STORY: BEING BULLIED

The bullying got so bad it felt like the whole school was out to get me for no reason. I felt anxious all the time. I'd wake up, remember I had to go to school and feel overwhelming panic. My mom took me to see a doctor, and I was diagnosed with anxiety disorder. I'm now seeing a counsellor, and the school is dealing with the bullies. Things are slowly improving.

WHAT TO DO IF YOU ARE BEING BULLIED

1. Tell someone. **NEVER** suffer in silence. You need to let a trusted adult know what's going on, so that they can help. And they **WILL** help.

2. Try and join in with others—maybe try some new after-school groups. Making new friends won't stop the bullying, but it can help you feel more positive and less alone.

3. Remind yourself that it's not you. This bullying is not your fault. It's the bully or bullies who are causing this. You are a wonderful, amazing person and you deserve to be happy.

4. Think big. It's hard, but try to remember that this is just one small part of your life, and that you have an exciting future ahead of you.

5. **TELL SOMEONE.** Did we already mention this one? Well, that's because it's the most important. You must must **MUST** speak up.

THE NOT-SO-REAL WORLD OF SOCIAL MEDIA

Social media is great. It's fun, and it keeps us connected to the world and our friends. It's also not real life. Think about it: what you see of someone online is just one small part of their life–the best part, the part they want people to see.

The same goes for celebs, YouTubers and any type of well-known person too. All humans have insecurities, can feel down, or have bad days. This part of life normally doesn't get displayed online.

Burst the social media bubble

If you're scrolling through social media and you start to feel bad about yourself, or wish that your life was better, STOP, and take a mindful moment. Close your eyes, take some deep breaths, and focus on nothing but your breathing. After 10 breaths, open your eyes, and list three things you love about your life, or are excited about doing in the future.

WORRY BUSTER

LIFE IS MORE THAN LIKES

How you appear on social media–and being popular too–can seem like the **MOST** important thing, and can affect how you feel about yourself. But life is so much more than likes, and worrying about what people think of you isn't a good use of your time.

1 Remember–people liking you in real life is **SO** much more important than getting those likes online.

2 Editing photos to make yourself look a certain way, or not letting people post photos where you don't think you look your best is creating a "fake" version of yourself. And if people don't like the real you, then what's the point?

3 Likes do not measure your worth. Your friends and family don't love you because you got 40 likes on that last Instagram post, do they? They love you because of all the little things that make you you.

4 Don't try to be anyone else. Walk your own path, and walk it tall–you are the best you that you can be!

DID YOU KNOW?

Looking at a screen (your phone, tablet etc) before bed makes it harder to fall asleep, and messes with your body clock! Do your brain a favor and stay away from social media for at least an hour before bed–you need proper rest to stay healthy.

SOCIAL MEDIA AND MENTAL HEALTH

Social media can sometimes harm our mental health. This may be because we start to judge ourselves in comparison to others we see online, or because of online bullying.

Online bullying, also called **"cyberbullying"** or **"trolling,"** is on the rise. Being cyberbullied is just as bad as being bullied in person. In fact, sometimes it can be **WORSE** because cyberbullies can bully their victims at any time of the day or night, and not being able to escape from that is awful.

Could you be a cyberbully without realizing it?
With this in mind, we **ALL** need to look into the social media mirror. Have you ever "liked" an unkind comment, or posted an embarrassing photo or video? Ever started or shared a rumor that could upset someone? Even if you meant it as just a bit of fun, this kind of behavior can be bullying.

Before you post or share anything, **ALWAYS** pause for a second and ask yourself: "How might this make someone else feel?" If you wouldn't like someone posting the same thing about you–**don't do it**.

IF IT'S HAPPENING TO YOU: 'STOP, BLOCK, TELL'

1 **Stop: log off.** The most helpful thing you can do is to get away from social media, and stay offline for a while. It's not a long-term solution–you deserve to use social media without being bullied–but while it's being sorted out, try to stay away.

2 **Use that block button.** Don't put up with nasty messages and comments–hit block.

3 **Tell someone.** Take screenshots, and tell a trusted adult, like a teacher. Schools have a responsibility to deal with cyberbullying just as much as physical bullying.

Here are some handy tips to keep yourself safe online.

1 Keep privacy settings **ON**, so only friends and family can see your posts.

2 Remember that what you post on the internet is out there forever! People can screenshot your pics, comments, or messages, even if you delete them later.

3 Don't add anyone you don't know. There are people out there who might pretend to be someone they're not to get close to you.

4 Never give **ANYONE** your personal information. This includes your address (that selfie you took in front of your house number is a big giveaway!), where you go to school, your surname, or your passwords.

PEER PRESSURE AND FITTING IN

What is peer pressure?

Your "peers" are your equals-people at the same level as you, like the people you go to school with. If they make you feel like you have to act a certain way or do certain things to fit in, that's called "peer pressure."

Some peer pressure is a good thing-encouraging someone to try a new sport, for example-but often peer pressure can be a pain.

EXAMPLES OF THE BAD KIND OF PEER PRESSURE INCLUDE:

1. Being pressured into skipping school.

2. Feeling like you have to join in with bullying, because you're scared if you don't, you might be next.

3. Being pressured to smoke cigarettes, drink alcohol, or take drugs.

4. Feeling pressured to have a boyfriend or girlfriend, or act a certain way around the opposite sex.

Coping with peer pressure

So what's the best way to cope with peer pressure? *You do YOU.* You're unique, you're amazing, and you should never change yourself for anyone. If they don't like it, they're not worth your time. You only have one life, and it's **YOURS**-be a strong and confident person who makes your own decisions and life choices. You're **NOT** a puppet on a string, you're the **SUPERHERO** in your own life. *cue dramatic music*.

Personal opinions and beliefs: embracing our differences

You know what would be sooooo boring? If we were all identical people, with identical thoughts and views. What makes the world so great is that we're all different—we come from different cultures, different backgrounds, we have different skin colors, speak different languages, have different opinions and beliefs... this uniqueness is what makes us human, and we should embrace it, and treat all people fairly.

Some people who are not so open-minded see someone different from themselves and think "I don't like them." These people are very **WRONG**. Do not be one of these people. Discrimination of any sort is plain wrong. Welcome the different with open arms... the best thing you can be is kind, and accepting. After all, don't you want people to be kind and accepting of you?

PEER PRESSURE: DRUGS AND ALCOHOL

Peer pressure can get really dangerous when it comes to alcohol and drugs.
A drug is something that changes the way we act or feel. Some drugs
(like aspirin or an inhaler) can help us, but others can do us real damage.
Drugs (including alcohol) can also have a serious impact on mental health—
especially when your brain and body are still developing—because
they affect both your body and your mind.

Q: What are illegal drugs?

A: Illegal drugs are drugs which
are against the law to have in your
possession or to use. Being caught
with an illegal drug is really serious
–and can get you in trouble
with the police.

Q: Alcohol isn't illegal though,
so does that mean it's OK?

A: It **IS** illegal for anyone under the age of 21
to buy it, and for good reason! Alcohol can be
enjoyed responsibly by grown-ups in small
doses, but too much can cause serious damage
to body and mind, and can lead to addiction or
dependence on alcohol, known as alcoholism.
Doctors now say that it is dangerous
for people under the age of 15 to
drink any alcohol, ever.

Q: What about cigarettes?

A: Cigarettes are packed full of harmful
chemicals and sticky tar that clog up lungs and
cause very serious health problems. They also
include a highly addictive substance called
nicotine, which makes it very hard to stop
smoking once you've started. Top tip:
never start! Nobody still thinks
that smoking is cool.

Q: What makes illegal
drugs dangerous?

A: Drugs can damage important organs in our bodies,
and can also affect our emotions. People who use
drugs often find it harder to think clearly and make
good decisions, and they may do risky or dangerous
things that could hurt themselves or others. A person
can even die from taking a drug just once. Drugs can
also lead to addiction, and addiction ruins lives, because
all the addict can think about is whatever it is they
are addicted to—instead of friends, family,
work, and all the important
things in life.

Q: Some kids in the year above
keep telling me I should try a drug called
cannabis with them. They've smoked weed before
and nothing bad happened. Should I do it?

A: Definitely not. Drugs cause different experiences
and reactions for different people. How a drug
will affect you can depend on many things like your
age, body type, your mental state, or where the
drugs are from. Just because someone else has
tried it and had a certain feeling doesn't
mean it will be the same
for you.

BOYS AND GIRLS: DIFFERENT BUT EQUAL

Boys and girls: they have different bodies, but does that mean they have to act differently? Sometimes we feel as if we do, and this can be a source of worry - like, will the other girls think I'm weird if I want to play football all day? Or, why am I crying, I'm a boy - shouldn't I be more manly?

FYI: the answer to both those questions is a big fat **NO WAY**. You can still enjoy the same things and experience the same emotions: we are all equal! Being equal doesn't mean that we're all exactly the same. We all have different strengths and weaknesses, likes and dislikes - but we have the same rights and opportunities!

Sexism sucks

When someone is treated unfairly, or expected to act a certain way just because of their sex, this is called sexism. For example, if a teacher told you that you weren't allowed to play football because you're a girl, that's sexism. Or if a woman is told she has to wear high heels to work, that's sexism too.

WHAT IS A FEMINIST?
....

It's really simple, actually. A feminist is anyone, male or female, who believes that males and females should be equal, and have exactly the same rights and opportunities in all areas of life. That's it!

Mental health and "manning up"

Sometimes, boys and men are expected to seem "manly" or "strong", and are told that they shouldn't cry or show emotion, because that's a "girly" thing to do. This is wrong, and can be very harmful to mental health. We have emotions for a reason, and they need to be expressed! If you need to cry, then cry—bottling up feelings inside will only make you feel worse. If you're a boy, never feel like you shouldn't talk about how you feel or problems you might be having —don't think that you have to "man up" and deal with things on your own.

SOME GIRL AND BOY DOS AND DON'TS

1. **DO** remember that girls and boys are equal, and just as capable of doing anything: whether it's sports, science, drawing, or baking. Anything!

2. **DON'T** use gender as an insult. Never say things like "You throw like a girl," "You're crying like a girl," "Man up," or "Grow a pair."

3. **DO** cry if you need to. It's normal for everyone – boys and girls-to cry when they're sad or overwhelmed: that doesn't make you weak, it makes you human.

APPEARANCE

BODY IMAGE

If you're reading this, chances are you have a body. Unless you're a floating head in a jar. Or a ghost. But what is "body image"? Body image is the picture of yourself that you have in your head, and the way you feel about yourself when you look in the mirror.

I can't go to the prom. I've got noBODY to go with!

Staying positive

Having a positive body image means truly accepting the way you are. It's not about being vain, or thinking you're better than others—it's about learning to accept everything that makes you you... whatever your shape, size, ethnicity, or gender.

This can be hard, especially while you are growing up, as your body is changing and can feel unfamiliar and awkward. But here's the thing. There is no "ideal," "normal," or "perfect" way to look. If you have a body, you are **beautiful**. And **amazing**. That's all there is to it.

Your body is the only one you have—so take care of it and love it, don't criticize or hate it!

4 WAYS TO BE BODY POSITIVE

1 **Don't compare yourself to others.** It's difficult, but try not to compare yourself to anyone else—classmates, siblings, or celebrities. Every one of us is unique, and that's **GOOD.** We should embrace our differences and individuality!

2 **Write down three things you like about yourself.** Your huge smile, your curly hair, your height, your toes... anything! Look at the list when you need a reminder of why it's great to be you.

3 **Treat yourself like a friend.** You don't sit looking for your friends' physical flaws, do you? Of course not. So don't do it to yourself. You love your friends and family because of who they are on the inside, not because of how they look—and the same goes for how they feel about you.

4 **Think positive.** If you realize you're having a negative thought about yourself, switch it up with some good vibes instead. Think about something you like about yourself, something you've done today that you're proud of, or something you did that made you happy. Being kind and accepting yourself is the most important thing you can learn to do in life (don't tell your math teacher we said that!).

BODY IMAGE, SELF-ESTEEM, AND MENTAL HEALTH

Your body image and self-esteem (that means your sense of your own worth, as a person) all start in the mind—not in the mirror. Having a healthy body image is a big part of mental well-being, because if you have a really negative opinion of yourself, it affects how you take care of yourself, both emotionally and physically.

Urrrghh, zits! I won't let them get me down, though...

If all you do is focus on what you don't like about yourself, it's easy to start feeling sad and negative about life in general. It also makes it harder to deal with new and difficult emotions or situations, because everything can be colored by the feeling "I'm not good enough." Focusing on the positive instead can be powerful.

Everyone has moments when they worry about how they look, but feeling depressed or obsessed about your appearance isn't healthy, and there is help and support out there.

Because you know what? You **ARE** good enough. You, person reading this, are a complex, one-of-a-kind human being, and you deserve to be happy. That's a fact. You can't argue. Nope, don't even try.

JAMIE'S STORY: LEARNING TO LOVE MYSELF

When I hit puberty, my appearance became everything to me. I hated how I looked—my body, my face, everything. I'd avoid mirrors, photos, anything that reminded me of how ugly I was. I'd constantly compare myself to friends and celebrities, and feel worthless. How come they looked like that, and I looked like **THIS?** I hated meeting new people—I just felt like they were judging me.

I spoke to my parents about wanting plastic surgery—I was only 15 at the time, and they were shocked by how I saw myself. They found me a counselor, and our appointments have been really helping. I'm not saying there's a quick fix, but recognizing that it wasn't healthy to be feeling that way was a huge first step.

READY, SET, GO: STAYING HEALTHY AND HAPPY

Taking care of your body is so important (we only get one, after all!) and –*bonus*– it's also a way of taking care of your mind. Staying active is a great way to stay healthy AND happy– because **exercise boosts your brain, too.**

First of all, **exercise increases your heart rate,** which pumps more oxygen to your brain, giving brain cells a boost. Nice. Second, it tells your body to release feel-good chemicals called **endorphins,** which improve your mood AND help brain development. Double whammy.

Some studies by super-clever science-type people have even shown that regular exercise can reduce the symptoms of anxiety and depression. Remember though, if you think you're struggling with either of these, you should see a doctor. Don't just hope that playing sports will solve everything.

DID YOU KNOW?

Humans weren't designed to be slumped on a sofa every day–we need to get our blood pumping, our HEARTS beating, and our MINDS soaring!

EATING DISORDERS

An eating disorder is an unhealthy relationship with food that can take over your life, make you very unwell, and even cause death. Anorexia is when someone stops eating almost completely. Bulimia is when someone eats a lot of food in a very short time (bingeing), then deliberately makes themselves sick.

Eating disorders are often related to something called "body dysmorphia." Having body dysmorphia means that someone might look in the mirror and see themselves as fat, no matter how thin they are or how much weight they lose. Eating disorders can also be about control, linked to other problems or issues someone is dealing with in life.

Eating disorders are forms of mental illness, and there are treatments that can help—you CAN recover. It can be very hard to admit you have a problem, but there are people who can help you. If

you think you may have an eating disorder, even if you aren't sure, talk to someone—a doctor, an adult you trust.... The first step is asking for help.

WHAT TO WEAR? FASHION AND BEAUTY

Finding your own style and expressing yourself through what you wear can be a big part of growing up. Dressing like your friends can be a way of bonding and feeling like you belong, and it's fun to try fashion trends together.

But it's not OK when you feel pressure to look a certain way to avoid being left out or picked on.

Q: I don't have the money to buy the kinds of clothes my friends are wearing, and it's making me feel really down. What should I do?

A: It can be really tough when you feel left out, but people are very wrapped up in their own lives, and are probably not even thinking about what you're wearing. You'll be worrying about it a lot more than they are, so try to focus on why your friends like you–it's your personality they want to hang out with, not your wardrobe.

Nice jeans!

Q: I'm 13 and I really want to wear makeup. I watch beauty tutorials on YouTube, but my parents REFUSE to let me buy any or try it. Why are they being so unfair?

A: Wearing makeup isn't a bad thing, but many schools will not allow it, so your parents might be concerned about you getting into trouble. They might also feel a bit scared and sad about you growing up... you are their baby after all! Try coming to a compromise, like getting a few bits of makeup, but not wearing it out unless they say it's OK. Also remember that there's no rush – eventually you'll be older, and will have years of experimenting with all the beauty products you want!

Q: I want to shave – is there an age it's OK to do that?

A: In terms of health, there's no reason why you can't shave, but always think about why you want to start. Do you really want to, or do you just want to fit in? You should speak to an adult before you start scraping away with a razor – you want to avoid an uncomfortable shaving rash (hint: always use a shaving cream or lotion) or painful little cuts (ouch!).

Everyone is entitled to dress how they want to, style their hair the way they want to, wear makeup how they like or not at all – individuality is a good thing, not something to be laughed at!

Wear what makes you feel comfortable, not what you think you "should" be wearing.

PUBERTY

DEALING WITH PUBERTY

Puberty isn't just about the physical transformation from child to–
AAARGH-grown-up! Your **BRAIN** is also developing, and that means
you get hit with a whole load of brand-new feelings and emotions too.

These new emotions can make puberty a seriously
overwhelming time. You might find yourself experiencing
mood swings, where you feel totally fine one minute, only
for something small to make you feel really sad or angry
a moment later. It can feel like being on a roller coaster.

The good news: it's **NORMAL.** This is one of the
most challenging times of your life in a lot of ways–
becoming an adult is a **BIG DEAL.** It's hardly surprising
that you might sometimes feel moody, sad, or
awkward and uncomfortable.

Puberty and mental health

While everyone will experience some level of mood swings during puberty, it's important not to confuse these with signs of mental ill-health. It's normal to feel irritable or down now and then, but if you're feeling sad all the time, or really struggling inside almost every day, you need help and support.

Never be afraid to talk to someone, and don't let anyone brush you off with "It's just hormones." Feel like your parent or teacher or whoever you've spoken to isn't taking you seriously? Speak to your doctor, or a school nurse—anyone. Only **YOU** know how you truly feel. If you feel like you need help, you need help. That's it.

DID YOU KNOW?

When you start puberty, your brain is changing along with your body. The biggest change happens in an area called the frontal lobe—the bit at the front of your brain that tells the rest of it what to do. It's not fully developed until you finish puberty, so as you get taller, grow pubic hair, start your periods (girls!), and all the rest, you'll also become more grown-up emotionally.

YOUR CHANGING BODY

Your body can be a big source of worry as you go through puberty, because not only is everything changing, but it's also virtually impossible not to compare yourself to others. At times it can feel like you don't even know your body anymore, and that's a lot to deal with. **One big worry buster? Remember that this is a process, and that growing up is a good thing!**

Q: I feel like all my friends are starting to develop, but I still look like a little kid. Is there something wrong with me?

A: No! Puberty is different for everyone. Most girls begin puberty between age 8 and 14, while for boys it's usually between 9 and 15, but both may start seeing changes earlier, or later. It happens when it happens, and there's nothing you can do to rush it or make it slow down… so don't panic, and remember–it all evens out in the end.

Q: I keep getting erections and I don't know how to stop it. Why is this happening to me?

A: Puberty knows how to make life hard, doesn't it? Erections are the male body's way of preparing for sex, but during puberty your body and brain haven't quite figured that out yet! Almost all boys will experience erections at totally random times, for no apparent reason. All you can do is wait for it to go away. Never try and force an erection down–you could damage your penis. Try carrying around a big folder, spare coat, or book for "cover-up" emergencies.

Q: How do I tell my mom that I want to start wearing a bra?

A: It can be tough talking about body-related things. But remember that all adults have been through puberty too, so they know a lot about how you're feeling. One good way of starting a conversation is to open with a simple "Can I talk to you about something?" Once that's out there, just get the words out and try not to feel embarrassed... your body is nothing to be ashamed of! If this sounds too hard, you could always try writing a little note. That way the worry is out in the open, and they can come and talk to you without you having to actually say the words.

Q: I'm growing hair everywhere–what's that about? It's really embarrassing!

A: First of all, there's nothing embarrassing about body hair–it's a totally normal feature that **ALL** humans have. When puberty hits, hair growth does too–popping up in places like your face, underarms, legs, and genitals (that's a fancy word for private parts). This is a natural part of becoming an adult. Body hair actually has loads of different uses, like keeping you warm and protecting your skin from germs.

FAMILY

SEPARATION AND DIVORCE

Two adults who love each other often decide to live together or get married, and have a family (that's where you come in!). But sometimes couples aren't making each other happy anymore, and they choose to live separately or end a marriage, which is called a divorce.

Adults splitting up isn't sad for just the grown-ups, but for the whole family as well, and it can be an incredibly painful and upsetting time. It might feel as though your world is falling apart, and that can make you feel angry, too.

There's nothing wrong with experiencing these emotions, but it's also important to understand that sometimes relationships end, and it's a sad but unavoidable part of life—even if it can be hard to cope with.

PRACTICAL WAYS TO COPE WITH DIVORCE

1. Remember that it's not your fault. Young people whose parents split up often blame themselves in some way, but you are not responsible. This is between them, not you.

2. Remind yourself that this doesn't change how they feel about you. Your parents will always love you, and divorce or separation won't change that.

3. Talk to your parents—they'll help you understand why this is happening. You could also chat with your brothers or sisters, friends, a school counselor, or a teacher. Just make sure you're not going through this alone.

4. Cry. You're allowed to cry. You're allowed to feel sad. You're allowed to feel how you feel. Equally, if you don't feel sad, that's fine too. It might be a relief. There is no wrong or right way to feel in this situation.

JANELLE'S STORY: COPING WITH A SPLIT

I was 10 years old when my parents told me that they were splitting up. It felt like my world was ending, and nothing would be normal again. I couldn't understand how we'd still be a family when my dad didn't live with us. Talking with them both helped a lot—they explained that I'd still see my dad every weekend and one night after school, and that I could stay with him whenever I wanted. It took some time, but we're all used to how life is now. It's different from how it was, but it's not worse. I know they both love me, and that's what is important.

OH BROTHER! SIBLINGS AND STUFF

Brothers and sisters can be your best friends one minute, then your worst enemies the next, right? But sometimes sibling problems can be more complicated than who ate the last cookie, or who's hogging the TV remote.

Q: My sister is so mean to me, I feel like she hates me. She's younger, but she's part of the "popular" group at our school, while I'm quieter. She's always making horrible comments, and it's really getting me down.

A: This is a form of bullying. She may be your sister, but that doesn't excuse her actions... if anything, it makes them worse. You need to speak to someone about what's going on—you should not have to deal with this, at school or at home. Can you talk to a parent? If not a parent, confide in a teacher or another relative or grown-up you trust.

Q: My parents are always comparing me to my older brother and I feel like I can't live up to him. They say things like "Matt never had any trouble with this," or "Why can't you be like Matt?" It makes me feel like a failure.

A: Being compared to a sibling is tough, and it's not really fair. We're all different and we all have our own strengths. Explain to your parents how these comments make you feel—they might not even realize that they're doing it. Another thing you can do is focus on your own strengths. Remind yourself of something you're good at, or enjoy doing, and remember that you don't have to be Matt.

Q: My parents got divorced a few years ago, and now my dad is marrying again. His new wife and three children will be coming to live with me and my dad and my brother. I don't really like the kids—how can I stop them from moving into my house?

A: Sometimes in life, things happen that are out of our control, and as much as you may want to, you can't stop this. Try talking to your dad and explaining that you feel a bit unsure about the change. When you're struggling in any way, talking to someone is the **BEST** thing you can do. It might help to remember that they're probably feeling strange about it all too... and you'll all need a while to get used to the new setup! Give yourself a few months for everything to settle before you judge them too much.

PARENTAL PRESSURE

Your parents just want the best for you. They want you to be happy, and do well, and to live the best life that you can. However, sometimes they can want so much for you that they end up piling on the pressure, and cause you stress or worry because you can't meet their expectations.

When help gets to be too much

Your dad might think that you're not being given enough homework, and sign you up for an after-school tutor, leaving you no time to see your friends, rest, or get away from the pressure of schoolwork.

Or your mom might be really proud that you're a good tennis player, and want you to practice all the time, even though you also need to study. This usually comes from a place of love, but it can be really hard to deal with. So what can you do?

PRACTICAL ADVICE

(1) You are only one person, and one person can only do so much. Try your best and do what you reasonably can, but don't let yourself feel guilty or like a failure because you can't do it all.

(2) Talk to your parents about your feelings. Calmly explain that while you realize they just want the best for you, it's causing you worry, and making you feel overwhelmed. If you feel like they won't listen, try speaking to a teacher, and see if they can talk to your parents with you.

(3) Make time for fun! Life isn't just about pushing yourself—you need balance, and that means time to relax and enjoy yourself.

(4) SLEEP. Sleep is so important, for your growing body and your developing mind.

AMIT'S STORY: FINDING WHAT I LIKE TO DO

My parents are both doctors. Ever since I can remember, they've wanted me to be a doctor too, even though what I really love is art. It felt like I didn't have a choice. They would always ask me why I wasn't studying, even when I'd finished all my homework. I felt like I couldn't relax.

In the end I spoke to my art teacher, who invited them in for a chat and showed them my work. It made them realize that I have other interests, and they've definitely stopped pushing so hard, but I still have to remind them that I need time to have fun, too. I'm so glad I spoke to someone.

LOVE AND RELATIONSHIPS

FIRST RELATIONSHIPS

Growing up and developing romantic feelings can be fun and exciting, but it can also come with a whole new set of worries! Worries like "Who do I like?" and "Who likes me?"

Having a crush

As you go through puberty, you'll probably develop feelings of attraction toward others. This is sometimes called "having a crush," which means liking someone–boy or girl, no matter what sex you are–in a romantic way. You might even want to be their boyfriend or girlfriend. (EEEK!)

Having a crush can be a bit scary and confusing. You want to know if they like you too; you don't quite know how to deal with these new feelings, and you just CAN'T STOP THINKING about them.

All of this is totally **normal** and **natural**, so you shouldn't feel like you have to hide your feelings. If you want to tell your crush that you like them, do it. If you don't, then don't. It's all about what you feel comfortable with.

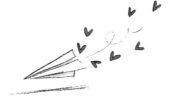

Oh, and P.S.: it's also fine if you DON'T like anyone in this way. There's no rule that says you have to like anyone that way.

WHAT A HEALTHY RELATIONSHIP LOOKS LIKE

Got a boyfriend or girlfriend? Great! But it's important that it's a healthy relationship. What does that look like? Like this:

1 **Trust.** It's OK to feel jealous once in a while, but you should trust each other enough to feel secure in your relationship. It's not healthy to feel you can't even talk to another boy or girl without your boyfriend or girlfriend getting upset or angry.

2 **Respect.** A partner should always respect you and your wishes. If you're feeling pressured into acting a certain way, or doing something you don't want to, that's unacceptable. Consent is essential in any relationship. (See page 60.)

3 **Equality.** A healthy relationship should be fair and equal. If one person gets their own way all the time, that's not OK.

4 **Time apart.** Yes, really! OK, so you're super into each other, but you both still have your own lives too. Don't forget to spend time with your friends!

DID YOU KNOW?

It's a normal part of growing up to have a crush on an older adult–it happens! What's **NEVER OK** is for an older adult to say or do anything that might encourage those feelings to grow.

UNREQUITED LOVE AND BEING DUMPED

First crushes and relationships are new, exciting, and fun, but what happens if someone you like doesn't like you back? What happens if you get dumped? The important thing to remember is that your world is not ending and that you will get through this.
Let's talk about some ways to cope with heartbreak.

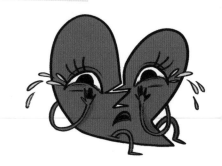

(1) **Do something fun with people you love**
Whether it's going to the park with friends or playing a game with your sibling, remind yourself that you are loved and that you have a life without this person!

(2) **Imagine your life in the future**
It can be easy to get caught up in a specific moment in time, so fast-forward and ask yourself: "Are you going to be feeling like this in five months time? How about five years? Will this person even matter then?" Give yourself some perspective–there will be many more crushes and relationships.

3. Pump that music

Forget the sad songs and put on your favorite upbeat track, **LOUD.** Now dance around your bedroom and sing along, even if you don't know the words. It **WILL** make you feel better!

4. Speak to someone

Do **NOT** go through this alone. Speak to a friend, a teacher, a parent, an uncle–it doesn't matter who it is, talking about your feelings is always a good thing, and bottling things up or trying to deal with things alone will only make you feel worse.

Q: I asked a boy in my class out and he said "No." The worst part is that he's told people he likes my friend Ashley. What's wrong with me?

A: There's nothing wrong with you. At all. Sadly, sometimes we like people who don't like us back, and it sucks. You put your heart on the line, and that was a really brave thing to do! We can't control how other people feel, but who they're attracted to is no reflection on us. Remember, you **WILL** feel better and you **WILL** have other relationships.

GENDER AND SEXUALITY

Sex and gender... what's the deal?

When you are born, doctors label you as a boy or a girl, based on whether you have a penis or a vagina. This is your **sex**. Your **gender** is your internal and personal sense of being male, female, or neither. It's about who **YOU** are and how you feel and behave.

So, what's sexuality?

Sexuality is different from gender. Your **sexuality**, or "sexual orientation," is who you feel attracted to, and want to have relationships with–in other words, who you like. There are different types of sexuality (see opposite page). It's something you are born with, and there is no right or wrong (that's really important to remember!). Only **YOU** can truly know your sexuality, because only you know how you feel.

Being transgender

Being transgender means that the boy or girl label given at birth doesn't match how someone feels on the inside. Many transgender people choose to change how their bodies are on the outside so that it matches how they feel on the inside. This is called "transitioning," and may include changing their name and the clothes they wear, taking hormones prescribed by a doctor, or having surgery.

It might take a while to discover your sexuality, and it can change over time. You might be attracted to boys when you're younger, then girls when you're older, or both. And you don't have to fit into one box! It's up to you to decide how you want to label yourself, if at all.

WORRY BUSTER

IN THE KNOW: WHAT MEANS WHAT?

Heterosexual/Straight: being attracted to the opposite sex–boys who like girls, and girls who like boys.

Homosexual/Gay/Lesbian: being attracted to the same sex–boys who like boys and girls who like girls. This is called being gay, or if you're female, being a lesbian.

Bisexual: being attracted to both males and females.

LGBT+: This stands for Lesbian, Gay, Bisexual, and Transgender, and the "+" sign represents all types of sexuality and gender identity that don't fit those labels. The "LGBT+ community" unites people under one supportive, inclusive banner.

SEXUALITY AND MENTAL HEALTH

Discovering your sexuality can be quite a journey, and it's not always easy—especially if you're also worried about how other people will react.

Some people have a hard time accepting anyone who isn't straight, and may even bully them because of it. In the United States and many other countries, it's illegal to treat someone badly because of their gender or sexuality, and it's never something you should have to put up with. It can have a serious impact on your emotional well-being and mental health.

Those who identify as LGBT+ are far more likely to suffer from mental health issues for a number of reasons. These reasons might include being bullied, or feeling different, alone, or misunderstood.

You should **never** feel like you have to deal with worries about sexuality by yourself. If you're feeling depressed, isolated, or like you can't cope, you must, must, MUST let someone know.

DID YOU KNOW?

The term "coming out" means deciding to openly describe yourself as gay, lesbian, bisexual, or another word that describes your sexuality. This usually also involves telling friends and family, but not necessarily everyone you know. It's up to you whom you tell, and when.

REMEMBER:

① **Accept Yourself.** Your sexuality and your gender identity are not a choice, and are definitely not a mental illness. You should never feel ashamed or embarrassed–it's your life, your emotions, and your feelings. Accepting who you are and learning to love yourself is **THE** most important thing you can do.

② **Know that you are not alone.** So many people have already been through what you are going through, and they are now living happy, healthy, and exciting lives. It's hard to figure it all out right away, but there is **ALWAYS** a bright future ahead of you.

③ **Be yourself.** Don't feel like you have to act a certain way because of your sexual orientation or gender. Yes, you might be gay, but that doesn't mean you have to start behaving differently– unless you want to. Do what makes you happy!

④ **Speak up.** If you're struggling with, or being bullied about, your sexuality or gender identity, speak to someone. There are also lots of help lines and websites that offer support and advice (see page 63).

SEX

Sex is a natural part of life–a private and intimate act between two adults, for both to enjoy. When you're growing up, it can seem a bit mysterious and secret, so it's normal to worry about what, why, and when–especially as your body and emotions develop and you start experiencing new sexual feelings.

What is sex, and why do people do it?
Sex is short for sexual intercourse, which is when two people take part in intimate acts involving their private parts. For a man and woman, sex can be when a man's erect penis goes into a woman's vagina. It's not "dirty" or anything to be ashamed about, but it's also important for both people to feel safe, happy, and respected. People have sex to make babies, but also because they enjoy it, and it's one physical way of being with someone that you love. Basically, sex should feel good!

Adults only

It's against the law to have sex before you're 16-18 years old, depending on the state. It's a step you should only take when you're mature and emotionally ready. Even when you are old enough, it's important to make sure that you are doing what **YOU** want to do, and not doing it to please someone else. You should never feel under pressure to have sex (or do anything intimate like kissing or touching) because you're worried a person won't like you if you don't, or because everyone else is doing it. Only you know when you're ready, and if you're not, everyone else needs to respect that. Of course, you don't have to wait until you're older to get more information or seek advice from a doctor, nurse, or clinic.

SEXTING

You should never feel pressured into doing anything intimate, and that includes sending sexual messages or sexual pictures (naked, or in underwear), which is sometimes called "sexting." It's actually illegal to take, have, or send a sexual picture of a child to anyone, ever—and if you're under 18, you're considered a child by law (even if you feel grown-up!). The other serious risk with sending private photos is that once they've left your phone, you don't know what the person you've sent them to might do with them, whom they might show them to, or who else might be able to find them. Even if it seems like everyone else is sexting, don't do it!

CONSENT AND CONTRACEPTION

When two people take part in any kind of sexual activity, and this even includes kissing, they both have to agree to what's happening. This is known as giving **consent**. And consent isn't just someone saying "yes" or "no"–it means paying attention to your partner and checking physical and emotional cues too.

This is super important: you can also stop at any time, or change your mind–and just because you agreed to one thing, it does NOT mean you've agreed to anything else! In the same way, just because you've done something before–even if it's with the same person–that doesn't mean you've consented to do it again. **Consent has to happen EVERY time.**

Let's talk about sex

CONSENT CHECKLIST

1 **Ask:** Only "yes" means "yes"–don't assume someone wants to do something just because they haven't actually said "no." It's as simple as asking "Do you want to do this?"

2 **Listen:** If someone says no, or that they're not ready, listen to them. Don't keep asking, or keep doing something in the hope that they will change their mind.

3 **Respect:** You should never make someone feel bad, or like they've done something wrong, if they say no. This is pressuring them into saying yes, and it's not OK.

Having sex responsibly

One of the big worries people have when they start having sex is about accidentally getting pregnant. Any time a man and woman have sex, they might make a baby-even if they don't want one-so it's essential that if you are a man and woman having sex, you use contraception.

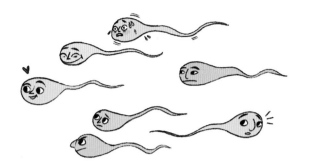

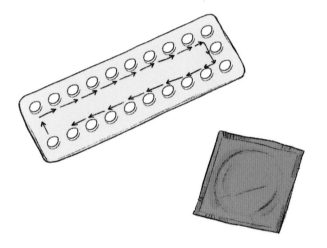

Contraception

Condoms and the pill are common forms of contraception. Condoms are made of latex and roll onto a man's erect penis to catch the sperm. The contraceptive pill is a tablet that a woman takes every day-it stops an egg from attaching to the lining of her uterus (womb). Some girls take the pill to help with painful periods or acne, even if they are not thinking of having sex.

Safer sex

Condoms protect both partners against most STIs (sexually transmitted infections). STIs are diseases that can be passed from person to person through sex. Using a condom is the best way to be safe, even if you are also using other contraception, and it is also very important for men having sex with men. You can find out more about contraception and STIs from your doctor or family planning clinic, or from the websites on page 63.

DID YOU KNOW?

There's also something called "emergency contraception," often known as the "morning-after pill." If a man and a woman have had sex and they didn't use contraception or something went wrong with it, they should see a doctor or pharmacist immediately, as this pill can stop a woman from becoming pregnant.

EMOTIONAL WELL-BEING

A positive sense of emotional well-being means that, as an individual, you are happy, confident, and able to meet everyday life head-on, feeling good about yourself both inside and out.

Hopefully this book has helped you to understand more about emotional well-being, and has given you some practical advice for dealing with the worries that come with growing up. GULP!

Life isn't always easy, but it also shouldn't be tough every single day. You deserve to be a **happy, confident** person, and **nobody** has a right to take that away from you.

Paying attention to your emotions and feelings is the first step to understanding your emotional well-being–so don't be afraid to feel, and don't be afraid to ask for help.

Everyone (adults included) can and should ask for help when they need it. Life can be hard for anyone and everyone at times, but we all deserve to be safe and happy. Face everything head on, and if you need some support down the road to adulthood and beyond, that's OK.

SUPPORT AND ADVICE

HELP LINES AND SUPPORT:

Child Helpline International
www.
childhelplineinternational.org

Kids Health
kidshealth.org
The Q&A section for kids will
help answer some of your
awkward questions.

stopbullying.gov
www.stopbullying.gov
Look for the section titled
"What Kids Can Do" for
advice on handling bullying.

The Trevor Project
www.thetrevorproject.org
1-866-488-7386
Help for LGBTQ youth

**CDC LGBT Youth
Resources**
www.cdc.gov/lgbthealth/
youth-resources.htm
Links to resources for LGBT
youth and supporters.

**LGBT National Help
Center**
www.glbthotline.org
Includes a national hotline and
youth talkline.

It Gets Better Project
itgetsbetter.org
Support for LGBTQ+ youth

MORE INFORMATION:

*Boys Guide to Becoming
a Teen* by Kate Gruenwald
Pfeifer (American Medical
Association, 2008)

Girl Talk and *Guy Talk*
by Lizzie Cox (QEB
Publishing, 2017)

*A Smart Girl's Guide
to Friendship Troubles*
by Patti Kelley Criswell
(American Girl, 2013)

INDEX